Medieval
CASTLES

© Aladdin Books Ltd 1989

Designed and produced by
Aladdin Books Ltd
70 Old Compton Street
London W1V 5PA

First published in
Great Britain in 1989 by
Gloucester Press
12a Golden Square
London W1R 4BA

ISBN 0 86313 928 0

Printed in Belgium

Back cover: A 15th-century drawing of the castle at Saumur.

Design: David West
Children's Book Design

Editor: Catherine Bradley

Illustrator: Rob Shone

Map: Aziz Khan

The author, Brian Adams, is the Keeper of Education
at the Verulaneum Museum, St Albans in England.

Contents

HISTORY HIGHLIGHTS
Medieval
CASTLES

GLOUCESTER PRESS
London · New York · Toronto · Sydney

INTRODUCTION

Castles can be found all over Europe. Some have become romantic ruins while others survive as grim reminders of how violent life was in the Medieval or Middle Ages. Medieval castles were built to protect those who lived in or near them from their enemies. The castles had to survive attacks so they had walls built round them. People lived in buildings within the walls.

Sometimes a bank and ditch were enough to put off an enemy. But when a country was taken over by another, the invaders needed castles to control their new lands. This happened in England in 1066 when the Normans (from Normandy in France) invaded. The Saxons (who had settled in England earlier) hated their new masters for seizing their land so they attacked the Normans. To establish their rule, the Normans built a network of castles. They were often built at river crossings, mountain passes or other important places.

The man with short hair on horseback is a Norman lord. He is about to go hunting with a hawk on his wrist. He is in charge and the long-haired Saxons are being forced to work for him. Behind him is his well built stone castle, where his family and soldiers lived.

DIFFERENT CASTLE TYPES

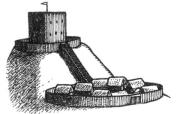

At first the Normans had wooden castles. They built a tower on a mound of earth (motte) with an open area round it (bailey).

Later castles were made of stone. They had a large stone tower or keep as well as a bailey. The walls were of stone with square towers.

Keeps were uncomfortable to live in so larger rooms were built within much stronger walls. Castles with two sets of walls were called concentric.

5

FIGHTING AND DEFENCES

Because castles were built to resist attack from an enemy, they had strong walls. As castles became larger, more than one set of walls were built. Beyond the walls there was a ditch or a moat. Moats were filled with water so that soldiers found it difficult to swim across. However it was easy to build a raft and float across the moat. So dry ditches were dug making it difficult for the attackers to get close to the walls.

When the men defending the castle started to fire arrows or stones, it became dangerous to attack the castle. If the attackers reached the walls, they would use long scaling ladders to climb over them. The defenders would then use long forked poles to push the ladders off. When the wall was taken, the defenders would move into the wall towers and continue the fight from there.

GATEWAYS

Wall towers had heavy wooden doors which were closed and barred when an attack began. Another defence was a portcullis. This was a heavy wooden and iron grating with spikes at the bottom. It was strengthened with plates of iron. To close it, the portcullis was lowered on chains by means of a winch put above it in the tower. The chains were wrapped round a large wooden roller turned by a wheel. Men working this wheel had to be strong as the whole thing was very heavy. You can still see slots and grooves cut into the stone gateways of many castles. These kept the portcullis in position and held it as it was being raised or lowered. The portcullis was part of the main gatehouse, which was heavily guarded.

As well as ladders, attackers used wooden siege towers. They had huge wheels so they could be moved up to the walls. If the attackers were too close to the walls the defenders would hurl rubbish or boiling water at them. Later castles had holes in the walls through which water – or boiling oil could be dropped.

7

keep

bailey

gateway

This castle has a square keep and walls built of stone. Near the walls were buildings such as stables, blacksmiths' forges – and even pig sties.

INSIDE THE KEEP

The large square keeps of the 12th century had to house soldiers as well as the lord of the castle and his family. The main room was the Great Hall where everybody ate. The lord sat on a raised platform or dais. His chapel was often near the hall while above was the private room where he and his wife lived. Below the hall were the ground floor rooms for the soldiers. This was a noisy area which also contained the kitchens.

Under the ground floor was the basement. Castle supplies were stored there. Prisoners were *not* put here! They were either made to work around the castle or kept in the smaller rooms upstairs. They were held until someone paid for their release.

Each floor had at least one large fireplace. Smoke escaped through special holes in the walls. These walls were really thick – over three metres in some castles. Notice the entrance stairs going up to the first floor. An attacker would have to fight up all these stairs to get into the keep. The well was dug inside the keep so that fresh water was available even in a siege.

In the keep the walls were made of stone and the floors of wood. The staircase for the keep was built so that the defenders had the advantage. They could use their swords more freely while the attackers could never really see their enemy. The lavatories were small rooms with chutes going down inside the walls to pits.

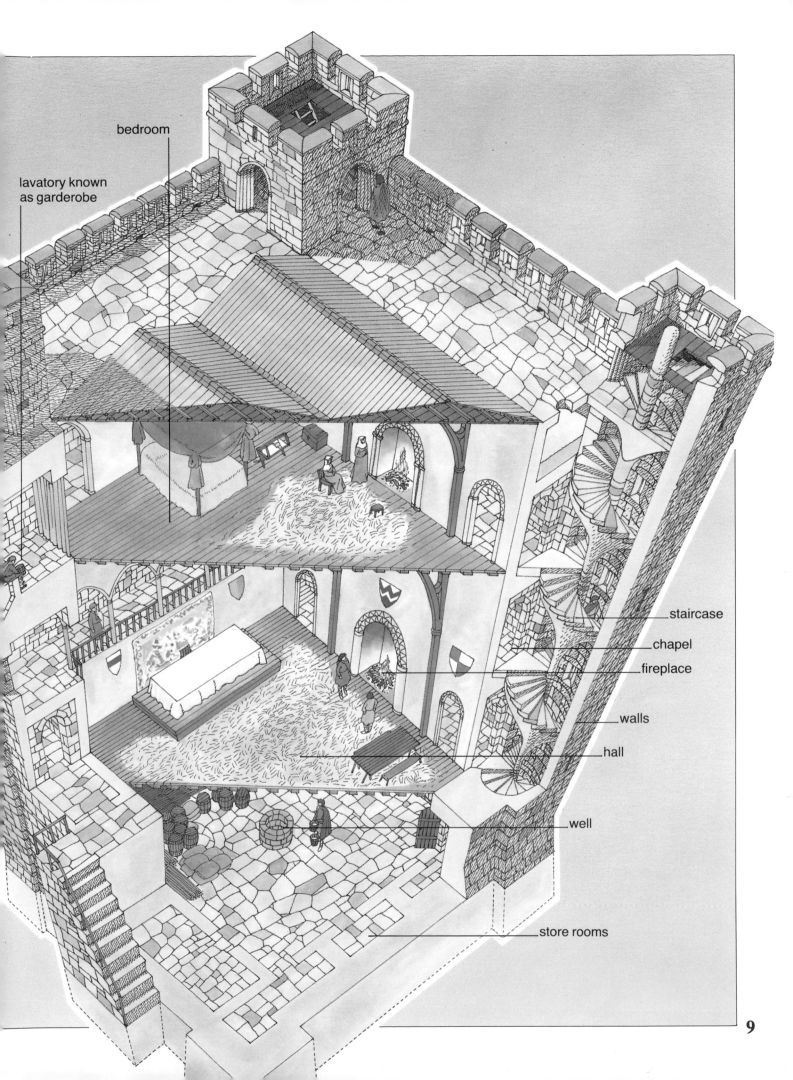

bedroom

lavatory known
as garderobe

staircase

chapel

fireplace

walls

hall

well

store rooms

QUEEN ELEANOR

Private rooms in castles were made more comfortable with wall hangings and tapestries. Furniture was very plain, but was covered with rich material. Lords took their furniture with them from one castle to another.

Eleanor of Aquitaine was married to the English king, Henry II. She was a lively and intelligent woman, who owned much land in France. She had been married to Louis VII of France but they were divorced by the Pope. This was most unusual at the time. She then married Henry. Henry was not the only one who wanted to control her lands. Queen Eleanor plotted against Henry with her sons. Henry won and kept her as a prisoner in various castles until he died in 1189. Then her son Richard, who had become king of England, released her. She lived for another 15 years.

The queen is shown in her private room. Henry kept her in great comfort. Here she is playing a game similar to the modern game of draughts. The pieces are made from walrus ivory. Around her she has servants and musicians.

King

Barons and church

Knights

Cottars

Villeins

Serfs

THE FEUDAL SYSTEM

Kings and queens were able to rule their countries by giving land to their followers in return for their services and taxes. Land was then passed down the feudal system. Everyone owed loyalty to the one who gave them land. The serfs had no land and were bound by law to their lords.

CASTLE PEOPLE

A medieval castle housed the lord and his family, his soldiers as well as the servants, who looked after them. In fact, the bailey was a very busy and crowded place.

There was a lot of work involved in running a castle. Blacksmiths or armourers were very important. They had to shoe horses, repair tools and look after the soldiers' armour. The soldiers patrolled the countryside on horses. They had to be looked after in stables. Carpenters made furniture and repaired carts. Other men looked after the buildings and repaired the walls. There was usually a plumber to make new lead roofs and pipes. "Plumber" means someone who works with lead.

Life in the Middle Ages was hard. People had to work very hard either growing food or in someone else's service. They did not live as long as they do today - many died of diseases, such as, the plague and others died in wars. A 40-year old was considered old.

COOKING IN A CASTLE

This is the kitchen at Glastonbury Abbey. Sometimes kitchens were built in the bailey. Several men worked in the kitchens preparing food. Food was obtained from the surrounding countryside but in a siege people had to survive on animals living within the bailey or on salted or dried food. Some castles had their own fishponds and dovecots. They provided fresh food throughout the year. Women rarely worked in the kitchen but they did wash the laundry. They had to make their own soap from animal fat and water mixed with vegetable ash. Candles were also made from animal fat.

13

GROWING UP IN A CASTLE

Children had a part to play in the life of a medieval castle. They fetched and carried and ran to deliver messages to people. However very few ever went to school. Clever boys would be taught by monks at a nearby monastery. Girls were usually taught how to cook and sew by their mothers. Richer families could afford to pay a teacher or tutor to educate all their children. In the poorer families, sons were trained by their fathers to do a job or craft.

Sons of noblemen were taught how to become soldiers and leaders in battle. They learned how to use weapons and were trained with wooden swords and shields. Some boys were sent to live in a powerful nobleman's house to learn leadership. They were called squires. Part of their training involved looking after their lord's armour, holding his horse for him to mount or carrying his food to him.

This covered wagon was used to carry women and young children on long journeys. A decorated covering was put over the wagon. It had no springs, so it must have been uncomfortable to travel in. Most adults went on horseback if possible.

TOYS AND GAMES

Children enjoyed games which are still popular. Boys played sports similar to bowls and football. They also rode hobby horses. Girls had wooden dolls to dress. Both girls and boys enjoyed hoodman blind where someone was blindfolded and tried to grab others in the game. Very young children had rattles and spun wooden tops.

BUILDING CHATEAU GAILLARD

Château Gaillard was built in France on a cliff overlooking the River Seine. Château means castle in French and Gaillard was built by Richard I of England in the 1190s. He put it there to protect his lands in France from attack. The castle had strong walls which divided it into sections. Each section had to be captured before the castle could be taken. The keep was round and less likely to be demolished in a siege. Richard had learned many lessons about defending castles in the Crusades in the Middle East. Gaillard was a new type of castle and looked very hard to attack.

Even so it was captured by the French king, Philip Augustus, in 1204. The French used towers and also undermined the walls. They got inside the castle after a soldier crawled up a lavatory chute. He helped the rest of the army get in by opening one of the windows. Shortly afterwards the English had to surrender.

Richard I saw to the building of Château Gaillard himself. It was built very quickly. Carpenters, masons and plumbers came from all over Normandy. Good timber and building stone from the area were brought to the site using horse drawn wagons. The cost for all the work was considerable.

DATE CHART

1189 Richard Coeur de Lion becomes King of England.

1195 Richard has to give his castle at Gisors to the French king, Philip Augustus. Decides to replace it with a new castle at Les Andelys near Rouen.

1197-98 Château Gaillard is built very quickly.

1199 King Richard is killed at Chalus by a crossbow arrow. John becomes King of England.

1203 August – Philip Augustus begins siege of Château Gaillard with a huge army.
  September – French build banks and ditches round the castle.

1204 February – French attack begins.

  March – The French finally capture Château Gaillard. This was an unusually long siege for a medieval castle. Towns sieges could last a lot longer.

1215 Philip Augustus adds strong towers to outer walls.

1300 Importance of Château Gaillard at an end. It is neglected and becomes a ruin.

Today the ruins of Château Gaillard are a national monument and have been heavily restored. They can be visited on the banks of the River Seine.

CASTLE SIEGES

Castles like Château Gaillard were built to resist attacks or sieges. Sieges were not always successful but they could go on for a long time. A siege usually only lasted a few weeks but in 1224 one lasted for three months. After that time, the food in the castle ran out and those inside had to surrender.

It was not always easy for the attackers. They had to camp in tents outside the walls until the castle surrendered. In summer both sides could be hit by disease. Sometimes the castle was relieved by soldiers friendly to those in the castle. This army would attack the besiegers' camp, set fire to their tents and drive them off.

Those under attack would also try to unnerve the enemy. They would throw bread off the walls to show that food was still plentiful. Dummies would be propped behind the defences to make it seem that there were more soldiers than there really were.

SIEGE EQUIPMENT

Stone walls could be undermined by using battering rams or climbed using a siege tower. Bits of wood were thrown into the ditch to fill it so that the tower could be pushed right up to the walls. Where the walls were large they were attacked with stones or fireballs. A fireball used burning materials to set fire to the timber parts of the castle. They were fired from a mangonel. This had a large timber piece shaped like a huge spoon. It was held down by twisted ropes. When the ropes were released, the timber shot up with great force and fired the missile. Sometimes even dead horses were thrown from these large catapult types of weapon.

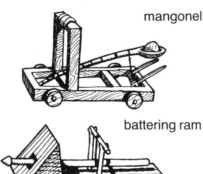

mangonel

battering ram

siege tower

A tunnel is being built under the wall. The tunnel is supported by timber. This would be set on fire when it had gone far enough in. The tunnel would then collapse bringing part of the wall down.

19

SAUMUR CASTLE

This beautiful castle looks over the town of Saumur in France. It was built by the Duc d'Anjou at the end of 14th century. A lot of money was spent on the building. There were gilded weathercocks, bell turrets and fine carved stonework. We know what Saumur looked like because it was painted in a book called *Les Très Riches Heures*. This was finished at about the same time as the castle. Around Saumur there are vineyards. Even today the area is famous for its fine wines.

LATER CASTLES

After about 1350 castles were no longer used just for defence. People wanted to live in greater comfort so new buildings were put up, sometimes within castle walls. There was also a new way of building, known as Gothic. The old style windows and doorways had been small with round arches at the top. The new Gothic windows had pointed arches and were much larger. They let in a lot more light. Glass was expensive and most windows were closed with wooden shutters or sheets made from horn.

Towards the end of the Middle Ages, some castles became very grand. They looked like fairy-tale castles with many pointed roofs and brightly painted walls. Fine stone carvings were put on arches and windows or on the walls. Rich people were becoming interested in gardens, planting roses and other flowers. The gardens had shrubs and trees cut into different shapes.

The people are waiting to see the lord of the castle. The man on the right is wearing a long sleeved gown and a hat based on Arab headgear. His wife has a hat with a net to tie in her hair. These clothes were fashionable about 1400.

TOURNAMENTS

The men taking part in a joust wore helmets with their crest or badge on top, so that everyone could tell who was fighting whom. Sometimes they wore a favour. This was a scarf or handkerchief belonging to a lady who favoured the man. The winner would present the favour to his lady, tied on his lance.

A tournament was a great occasion, which often went on for several days. It was usually held outside the castle and attracted lots of visitors. The main event was the joust. Two men would charge each other on horseback. Both wore armour and their horses were covered in richly embroidered cloth. The men held long blunt wooden lances and would try to knock each other down. Since the lances were very heavy this needed a lot of skill. They did not try to kill each other but usually everybody ended up badly bruised. Apart from jousting, there were also archery competitions, wrestling matches and sword fights at a tournament.

Tournaments began in France in about 1050 when several men took part in pretend battles. Since these were dangerous and men were killed, single combat took its place. The tournament was ideal for men to practise fighting and prove how skilled they were.

THE AGE OF CHIVALRY

This period in history is called the Age of Chivalry. You could succeed in life if you followed the rules of chivalry. Honour and fair play were taken very seriously. When a man wished to marry a woman, there were rules to follow. Men would write poems to the women they loved and try to win their love. This was known as courtly love. If a man loved someone else's woman, one way to settle the argument was to take part in a tournament.

FEASTS

Feasting and enjoying food was very important in the Middle Ages. At times, food was scarce for everybody, not just the poor. Bread was the basic food. It could be made from barley and rye as well as wheat. The wealthy used thick slices of brown bread as plates to eat on. They were called trenchers. Next to bread, fish was the most common food. Usually fish was salted or pickled to preserve it. Birds like chickens, ducks or geese were popular. On special occasions the better off ate swan and peacock. Beef and venison (from deer) were well liked, and pigs were kept for pork.

In the castle gardens, vegetables like cabbage and leeks would be grown. Herbs were used to season food or make remedies when people fell ill. During the Middle Ages new foods, such as raisins, dates and figs, were brought to Europe by the Crusaders. Before 1100 the only way to sweeten food was with honey. Spices were very expensive because they came all the way from the Far East.

Most people used their fingers to eat their food. Forks were brought in towards the end of the Middle Ages. Many people thought that using forks was silly but everyone had to behave properly at mealtimes. There were many rules on the correct way to eat and where people had to sit at the table.

EATING

The castle kitchen was quite far from the great hall so that the smell of cooking was kept away. Some castles had a small kitchen near the hall where food was reheated. This is a reconstructed medieval kitchen at Cotehele in Devon, England.

Food was cooked in metal pots called cauldrons. Meat was roasted on large spits over a fire. Since glass was too expensive, food was stored in pots or wooden barrels. The rich had bowls made of pewter or even cups of silver and gold. Plates were rarely used.

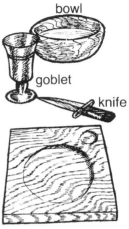

bowl

goblet

knife

wooden board

WHAT HAPPENED TO CASTLES?

As the Middle Ages came to an end, strongly defended castles became out of date. A few well-aimed shots from a cannon could easily knock a wall down. This was shown very clearly during 17th century wars. In central Europe the Thirty Years' War began in 1618 while in England the Civil War began in 1642. Both wars were very bloody and caused terrible damage.

In England, Oliver Cromwell's army was well organised. The soldiers had the latest type of armour and used the most powerful cannons available. However, it was not always easy to capture the larger castles. With their many towers and enormously thick walls, a lot of ammunition was used. The castles had to be captured one by one. Pembroke Castle in Wales was attacked by Cromwell himself in 1648. The siege lasted from 22 May to 11 July, when the big guns had destroyed its walls.

Cromwell's army attacks one of King Charles I's castles during the English Civil War. Many castles were badly damaged during the war. If they were too expensive to repair, they were abandoned. Only castles which were still used by the army, like Dover, were kept in good condition. They were altered as new types of defence came in.

NEW DESIGNS

Tilbury Fort was built in the 15th century on the mouth of the River Thames. In the 17th century, it had new walls built according to the new designs.

They were very thick to withstand cannon fire. The walls stuck out so that the defender's cannons had a clear firing area.

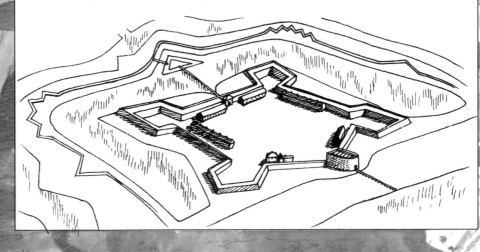

CASTLES WORLDWIDE

Castles were not just built in Europe. They are found throughout the world. Ch'ang-an in China, for example, was a huge rectangle over 9 km wide and 8.4 km from north to south. It was built in the 7th and 8th centuries by the T'ang emperors. Within its walls was the emperor's palace, which had its own walls. Ch'ang-an was as large as Baghdad in Iraq, which was probably the largest city in the Middle Ages.

The Kremlin in Moscow, in the Soviet Union, has 19 towers and pink coloured walls almost 20 m high. It was built in the 15th century for the Russian Tsars. Inside there are palaces and several beautiful churches. Today, the Kremlin is used to house ministries and government offices.

Further west, in Germany and Poland, castles were built by powerful men called the Teutonic Knights. The German emperor also built castles to defend his lands. In other parts of Germany and Switzerland important men also built castles. Many of these are now museums or tourist attractions.

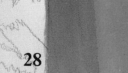

JAPANESE CASTLES

This is Himeji castle in Japan. Castles there were built mainly of stone. They were quite simple pavilions built for the emperor. After the 16th century they had thick, high walls. Because of earthquakes in Japan, the walls curved inwards and were strengthened at the base and corners. This was to stand up to the shock of the earthquake. The palaces of the emperors or Shogun warlords had outer defence works. Nearly all of them had moats.

This impressive site is in southern Africa. The ruins are called the Great Zimbabwe. They were built after 1200. The stone walls were beautifully made and were more for show than defence.

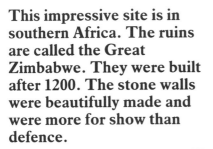

DATE CHARTS

1066 AD The Normans under Duke William conquer England. Wooden castles are built. Tower of London is started in stone.

1086 Domesday Survey carried out.

1100 About 500 castles in England.

c1100 Great Zimbabwe in Africa began.

1150 Stone castles are built with rectangular keeps.

1154 Henry II is king of England and rules Aquitaine.

1180 Castle with square wall towers are built.

1200 Castles with round wall towers are built.

1271 Great Crusader castle of Krak des Chevaliers, Syria, falls to the Arabs.

1280s Concentric castles built by Edward I in England.

1295 War in Wales. Major Welsh castles built.

1370s Cannons begin to make castles dangerous to defend.

1337 Hundred Years War between France and England.

1346 Battle of Crécy. Decline in importance of castles.

1429 Joan of Arc begins French defeat of English in France. Castles built for show not defence.

1520s End of medieval castles and development of new forts.

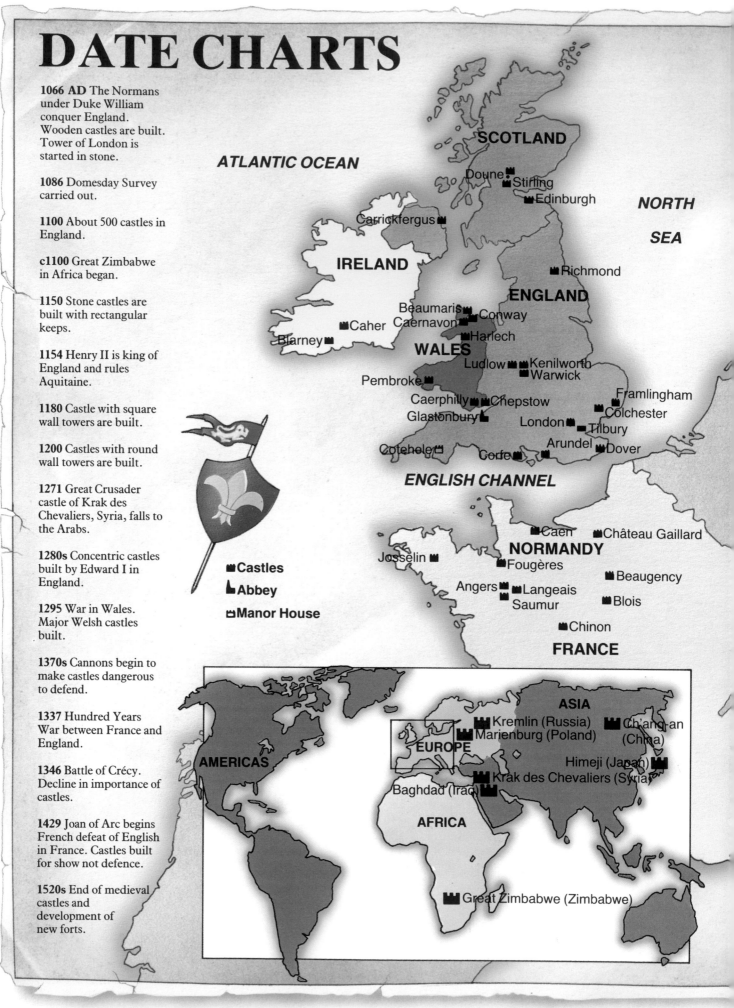

ATLANTIC OCEAN

SCOTLAND

NORTH SEA

Doune ♜ Stirling
♜ Edinburgh

Carrickfergus ♜

IRELAND

♜ Richmond

ENGLAND

Beaumaris ♜ Conway
Caernavon ♜
♜ Caher
♜ Harlech

Blarney ♜

WALES

Ludlow ♜ ♜♜ Kenilworth
♜ Warwick

Pembroke ♜

Framlingham ♜
Caerphilly ♜ ♜ Chepstow
Glastonbury ♱
♜ Colchester

London ♜
Tilbury ♜

Cotehele ⌂

Arundel ♜
Corfe ♜ Dover ♜

ENGLISH CHANNEL

♜ Caen ♜ Château Gaillard

Josselin ♜

NORMANDY

Fougères ♜

♜ Beaugency

Angers ♜ ♜ Langeais
Saumur

♜ Blois

Chinon ♜

FRANCE

♜ **Castles**
♱ **Abbey**
⌂ **Manor House**

ASIA

♜ Kremlin (Russia)
♜ Marienburg (Poland)

♜ Ch'ang-an (China)

EUROPE

Himeji (Japan) ♜

Baghdad (Iraq) ♜ ♜ Krak des Chevaliers (Syria)

AMERICAS

AFRICA

♜ Great Zimbabwe (Zimbabwe)

30

AFRICA	ASIA	AMERICA	EUROPE
		500 AD Beginning of Mayan civilization in central America. Development of Teotihuacan.	**By 500** Roman empire in Western Europe has collapsed and is overrun by barbarians.
641 AD Arabs take over Egypt and overrun North Africa.	**618 AD** Establishment of T'ang Dynasty in China		
700 Arab traders set up trading settlements in East Africa. Coptic Christians in Ethiopia.	**751** Arabs defeat Chinese in central Asia.		**800** Charlemagne crowned emperor in the West. Vikings from Scandinavia attack British Isles. Beginning of the feudal system.
800 The kingdom of ancient Ghana trading across to the Sudan.	**907** End of T'ang Dynasty.		**911** Vikings (Norsemen) allowed to settle in Normandy. They become Normans.
	960 Sung Dynasty in China.	**980** Toltec capital set up at Tula (Mexico)	
1054 Ghana conquered by Almoravid Berbers from the north.	**c1000** Gunpowder in China.		**1066** Norman conquest of England.
			1073 Gregory VII Pope. Quarrel between him and German emperor Henry IV as to who controls the church. Settled 1122.
c1100 Beginning of the building of the Great Zimbabwe. Growth of the kingdom of Ife in Nigeria.	**1210** Mongols invade China under Genghis Khan.	**1151** Fall of Toltec empire.	**1096** First Crusade.
			1295 First representative parliament in England called by Edward I.
	1279 Sung Dynasty falls to the Mongols.		**1314** Poland is reunited following Mongol raids.
		1350 Beginning of Aztec empire, becoming independent after 1428.	**1348** Black Death (Bubonic Plague) sweeps across Europe.
	1368 Ming Dynasty in China takes over from the Yuan Dynasty.		**1378** Rival popes at Rome and Avignon in Great Schism (to 1417).
1400 Decline of Zimbabwe. Growth of state of Benin. In southern-central Africa kingdom of Great Bantu develops.			**1410** Poles and Lithuanians defeat Teutonic knights from Germany.
			1415 English victory over French at Agincourt, during Hundred Years War (began 1337).
	1421 Peking (Beijing) becomes capital of China.	**1438** Inca empire in Peru expands.	**1429** French begin reconquest of France.
		1450 Incas conquer kingdom of Chimu.	**c1450** First printing press, in Germany, during the Renaissance (a rebirth of learning and art throughout Europe)
		1521 Cortés conquers Tenochtitlàn.	
		1533 Pizarro brings down Inca empire.	**1500** Gradual end of Middle Ages.

INDEX

Photographic Credits:
pages 7, 13 and 20: The Ancient Art and Architecture Collection/Ronald Sheridan; page 17: Michael Holford; page 25: National Trust Picture Library; page 29: Hutchison Library; back cover: Bridgeman Art Library.

PRINTED IN BELGIUM BY
proost
INTERNATIONAL BOOK PRODUCTION